D1583054

TROG: FORTY GRAPHIC YEARS

FORTY GRAPHIC YEARS

The Art of Wally Fawkes

FOREWORD BY RAYMOND BRIGGS

INTRODUCTION AND COMMENTARY BY FRANK WHITFORD

FOURTH ESTATE · LONDON

First published in Great Britain in 1987 by
Fourth Estate Ltd
113 Westbourne Grove
London W2 4UP

Illustrations © Wally Fawkes
Text © Frank Whitford

BRITISH LIBRARY CATALOGUING IN PUBLICATION DATA

Trog
    Trog : forty graphic years : the art of
Wally Fawkes.
    1. Canadian wit and humor, Pictorial
I. Title II. Whitford, Frank
    741.5'971   NC1449

ISBN 0-947795-17-0

The publishers wish to thank the Daily Mail for permission to reproduce
the episode of 'Flook' appearing on pages 38-54.

Designed by Peter Ward
Typeset in Bodoni by Lithoflow Limited, London
Printed and bound in Great Britain by
The Bath Press, Bath, Avon

CONTENTS

FOREWORD

Wally Fawkes is one of the world's greatest living cartoonists and it is a sad reflection of the status of cartooning in Britain that his admirers have had to wait over a quarter of a century for a major book of his work. On the continent he would have been lionised for decades. The work of Hergé, the creator of Tintin, has been available in massive, four-hundred-page volumes for many years. Yet Britain, despite its tradition of cartooning from Gillray and Rowlandson to Low, Giles and Trog, seems to undervalue its own artists and to turn its snobbish cultural back on them. This is particularly true of British strip cartoons which are reprinted regularly in book form on the continent but not in Britain.

But the remarkable thing about Wally Fawkes is that he is not only a brilliant strip artist, but a great political cartoonist and a superb caricaturist as well. It is an extraordinary combination of skills possessed by no one else anywhere.

There is also his phenomenal energy to consider. Anyone who works in this field knows the enormous amount of time the work takes and how easily it can become tired and mechanical. In over forty years Wally Fawkes seems never to have flagged. There is an unfailing quality of *enjoyment* in his drawing, a pleasure in getting it finished, neat and complete, and in getting it crystal clear and *right*. There is an astonishingly sharp focus too, particularly in the caricature, which makes the characters seem larger than life, as if seen under a brilliant light and a powerful lens. Then there is the quality of his blacks, which seem to be blacker than black. Does he use the same ink as the rest of us? How does he do it? How does he keep going? Where does his energy come from? Is it the jazz? Perhaps the Clarinet is Good For You?

May Trog continue to delight his public and baffle his fellow artists for many years to come. This book is long overdue.

RAYMOND BRIGGS, 1987

INTRODUCTION

Self-portrait

Dead are the days when the major attraction of *Punch* was its full-page political cartoon, when the importance of political cartoonists for the circulation of newspapers was reflected in their considerable salaries and perks and when a political cartoonist like Bernard Partridge or David Low could be knighted.

Newspapers, like *Punch*, have changed and, in Britain at least, the few political cartoonists in the traditional mould are now far outnumbered by the social commentators and observers of the whimsy and trivia of everyday life. Giles is the old master of this highly popular and, as far as the health of the political cartoon is concerned, suffocating genre.

The British political cartoon has not given up the ghost, however. It lives on in the work of a small number of variously gifted artists of whom Trog is the longest-serving and universally regarded as the best.

No cartoon is easy to conceive or draw. But the successful political cartoon is a more difficult form than any other because of the way word and image need to be concentrated within a telling unity. There is no room for fanciful rambling, for interesting but inessential detail. Everything must be distilled, be as pure and potent as an aphorism. And it must be as elegantly turned.

According to Trog, making a political cartoon is like writing a play whose action, conflict and development of character is condensed into a single line. He also believes that the political cartoon is uniquely dependent on caricature. Caricature in turn depends on graphic skills of a very high order, skills which are not taught at art schools any more, where — for a time at least: there are current signs of reaction — the plaster casts were removed from the antique rooms and life drawing found no place in the curriculum.

Old-fashioned skills were taught at Sidcup Art School, however, when Wally Fawkes, not yet in possession of his *nom de plume*, enrolled there as a student in 1938 at the age of fourteen. It was the art school closest to his home in Kent where he had lived since coming to England with his family from Vancouver in 1931. During the eight months he studied there he developed a taste for the discipline and concentrated observation demanded by drawing both from the antique and from life.

1. *Interview with the author, 30 July 1987*

2. *ibid.*

3. *Leslie Gilbert Illingworth (born Barry, South Wales 1902, died, Robertsbrige, Sussex 1979); abandoned studies at the Royal College of Art in London to join the* Western Mail *as cartoonist in 1920. First published in* Punch *1926. Cartoonist for the* Daily Mail *1939-1968. Took over from Bernard Partridge as political cartoonist in* Punch *in 1945.*

His tutors regarded him as highly promising and they were as disappointed as he when financial difficulties obliged him to abandon his studies and look for work. War had been declared and Fawkes found employment painting camouflage in a factory at Woolwich. He used to cycle there from his home in Sidcup every day until the factory was bombed, an event which the cartoonist describes as 'the harshest criticism' his work had ever received up to that time.[1]

A position drawing maps and diagrams for the Coal Commission followed, and although the offices were situated in Victoria, Fawkes used to cycle there every day. While he was working there an art competition for Commission employees was announced and Fawkes decided to enter what he remembers as a 'colour wash drawing of a boxer stepping into the ring, about to enter the spotlight and obviously keyed-up'.[2] He thought so little of his chances that, instead of staying for the judging which took place during the lunch-break, he went off to buy some Louis Armstrong records. When he returned he discovered that he had won first prize. He had also missed meeting the judge, the distinguished *Daily Mail* cartoonist Leslie Illingworth.[3]

Illingworth sensed so much promise in the drawing of the boxer that he remembered Fawkes's name and soon contacted the young artist, offering to find him a position better suited to his talents in a commercial art studio. Later — in 1945 — Illingworth, by then a friend, arranged for Fawkes to be employed by his own paper, the *Daily Mail*, as a graphic artist, producing column-breakers and other decorative illustrations for news and feature pages. Fawkes arrived at the *Mail* on his twenty-first birthday.

It was not the first time he had been to Fleet Street. In his last year at school he had won a competition organised by the *News Chronicle* for outstanding cricketing performances and had visited the paper's offices to receive as a prize a signed bat from Jack Hobbs. That occasion was memorable enough (Fawkes, a member of the MCC and a regular visitor to Lords, remains a cricket fanatic), but his arrival at the *Mail* to work as an artist for a great national newspaper was the fulfilment of a dream.

Fawkes, who adopted the pen-name Trog almost immediately, was connected with the *Daily Mail* for more than thirty years. He drew column-breakers, then produced a daily comic strip and eventually became the paper's chief political cartoonist.

Fawkes's decision to hide behind the monosyllabic alias Trog had something to do with the then current fashion for cartoonists to adopt simple and memorable signatures ('Sprod' is the example that springs most readily to mind), but it was probably more the product of a distaste for self-advertisement, of a reticence to talk about himself which he continues to this day.

Fawkes borrowed the name Trog from a jazz band. Shortly before the end of the war he had begun to play the clarinet in the George Webb Dixielanders, a group which, since it frequently performed in cellars and other subterranean venues, quickly became known as 'The Troglodytes'. Soon after he rechristened himself for publication purposes he developed the characteristic dot-and-carry signature which he still uses.

THE MUSICIAN

Wally Fawkes is an outstanding jazz musician, according to some one of the greatest clarinetists Britain has ever produced and in the opinion of the virtuoso Sidney Bechet, one of the best in the world. Between 1948 and 1956 when he performed regularly with the Humphrey Lyttleton band, he was indeed better known as a musician than as an artist. Today he plays less often but, as he puts it himself, 'the cartoonists know me as the one who plays the clarinet. The jazz people say I'm the one who does the cartoons.'[4]

In love with jazz, especially of the New Orleans variety, from an early age, Fawkes decided to take up an instrument in 1942. He bought a clarinet and an instruction manual ('which taught me to blow down the narrow end and technical details like that'[5]) and was making rapid progress until pleurisy obliged him to spend two months in hospital. Anxious that his lungs would remain too weak for him ever to play again, he was relieved when his doctor assured him that practising the clarinet would be ideal therapy.

In 1944 he became a founder-member of the George Webb band which was at first entirely amateur. The jazz critic Max Jones remembered making 'the pilgrimage to The Red Barn in Barnehurst to marvel at the unfamiliar, enjoyable raw sounds ... rendered

Leslie Illingworth

4. *quoted after Max Jones, 'Trog as Musician' in* Flook at 30, *exhibition catalogue, Centre for the Study of Cartoons and Caricature, University of Kent at Canterbury, 1979, p8*

5. *Interview*

Illingworth's portrait of the cartoonist and clarinetist

6. *Max Jones, op. cit.*

with forceful inaccuracy by pianist George Webb ... my favourite bandsman was the clarinetist Wally Fawkes. He had a feel for the clarinet, and obvious if embryonic talent, and a warmth in his playing which particularly made up for a tendency to blow out of tune much of the time.'[6]

After the war the band acquired a new trumpeter, an unlikely combination of Old Etonian, former Guards officer and current art student. This was Humphrey Lyttleton who in 1948 founded his own group with Fawkes as a key member. It rapidly became famous, enjoying the kind of adulation accorded now only to rock-stars — although Fawkes points out that traditional jazz only ever appealed to a minority and was never as popular as the music of, for example, Johnny Ray. Nethertheless its concerts were sold out weeks in advance (the band was frequently obliged to give to concerts a night to accommodate the crowds) and such records as 'Bad Penny Blues' made it to the hit parade.

Yet Fawkes never abandoned his position at the *Daily Mail* in order to become a full-time musician. He somehow managed to combine his drawing with regular concert work.

It was not only the extraordinary pressure of such a double and peripatetic life which eventually forced him to stop performing with the Lyttleton band. In 1956 he reluctantly left it partly because of what he admits were 'the horrors of appearing on concert platforms.'[7] Huge audiences had begun to give him claustrophobia and even the ability temporarily to lose himself, to drown his self-consciousness in bursts of spontaneous, lyrical improvisation was not enough to enable him to conquer his innate shyness.

7. *Interview*

He felt more at ease with smaller audiences and for about three years in the late 1950s worked with his own band, inevitably called The Troglodytes, at venues less intimidating than concert halls. Since the Troglodytes broke up Fawkes has not played in public more than two or three times a week — he joins various bands as a guest performer whenever he can and sometimes performs with Humphrey Lyttleton. Fawkes's low profile is regretted by his many admirers who, like Max Jones, are entranced by his 'personal sound (a vibrant and moving tone) and richly melodic style'.[8]

8. *Max Jones, op. cit.*

The studio at Fawkes's North London home contains not only the usual clutter of the working cartoonist but also musical instruments. One desk is littered with pens, brushes, bottles of ink and pots of paint while arranged on another are reeds for his clarinet and soprano saxophone. He obviously takes great delight in playing ('It's sheer pleasure; no one could ever describe drawing to a deadline as a pleasure') and does not admit to practising. When someone asked him how much he practised, he replied: 'Practise? I'm not good enough to practise — I just play tunes.'[9]

9. *Interview*

Curiously, Britain has produced many musicians with a talent for the visual arts. In recent years popular performers as diverse as several members of the Beatles, the Who and Ian Dury began their careers at art school and several of the jazzmen who came to prominence in the 1950s had a similar background. One of Humphrey Lyttleton's contemporaries at the Camberwell School of Art was the clarinetist Monty Sunshine and the guitarist Diz Disley earned part of his living making illustrations for record covers and music magazines.

Fawkes, when pressed, sees connections between playing jazz and making cartoons, or rather between jazz improvisation and caricature. It is, he says, 'a matter of inventing variations which bring out rather than mask the original melody, which comment on its essential qualities. The bone structure of a face is like the chord sequence which underpins a melody. You can't play — or draw — anything which distorts or destroys that fundamental structure.' He adds that much modern jazz makes him think that the performers have never been anywhere near an art school: 'I may be deaf, but it sounds to me like a lot of musical scribbling.'[10]

10. *ibid.*

There are more obvious connections between Fawkes the musician and Trog the artist. Many of his collaborators on cartoons have been friends from the world of jazz. Humphrey Lyttleton wrote some of the scripts for 'Flook', the strip with Trog made his name, and the writer and blues singer George Melly not only wrote 'Flook' for many years but also provided the ideas for Trog's earliest political cartoons.

EARLY WORK

Leslie Illingworth was the first to recognise Fawkes's talent as an artist. He had arranged for his appointment to the *Daily Mail* and he exerted a crucial influence on his early work.

Illingworth was a Welshman who, seemingly unaware of his prodigious gifts as a draughtsman and unaffected by his reputation as one of the world's best cartoonists, selflessly encouraged younger artists (and potential rivals) and derived genuine pleasure from their success. Trog remained a close friend of Illingworth until his death in 1979: one of the few photographs in his studio is of the artist from whom he learned so much and of whom he painted a marvellously expressive portrait in the year of his death.

Throughout his career Trog has revealed his admiration of Illingworth by alluding

Fawkes's portrait of the artist as a young man
c. 1955

'ONCE MORE INTO THE SHIT...'

Fawkes imitates Illingworth (*Private Eye*, 1964)

to him in his work. For a special issue of *Private Eye* that satirised *Punch* Trog produced a political cartoon in the manner of Illingworth; and in an episode of 'Flook' which dealt with the controversial arrival of West German tanks in Wales for training, he introduced as the leading character an aged ARP warden living in a cave who refused to believe that the war was over. He was Leslie Illingworth to the life — in attitude as well as looks.

During Trog's early days at the *Daily Mail* Illingworth was more than a help: he was an inspiration. A superb artist (he had studied at the Royal College of Art) with a deep understanding of the peculiar demands made by drawing for reproduction and a dislike of the short-cuts taken by most of his colleagues, he taught Trog about techniques and materials and communicated an enthusiasm for craftsmanship for its own sake.

Trog copied Illingworth's work ceaselessly, sometimes reproducing one of his friend's drawings line for line. He imitated his elaborate cross-hatching and the way he built up his drawings in terms of carefully judged half-tones. He even learned how to use scraperboard which Illingworth was among the first cartoonists to employ. Many of Trog's miniature graphics for the *Daily Mail*, among them the illustration reproduced here, were in this difficult medium.

Trog became so adept at imitating Illingworth that he once carried out a piece of work for him. Too busy to meet the deadline for an advertising strip commissioned by the Central Office of Information, Illingworth asked Trog to draw it for him. It was such an excellent pastiche that the COI found it difficult to believe that Illingworth had not made it himself.

In spite of the debt to Illingworth the influence of a few other artists is discernible in Trog's early work: Ronald Searle, Pearl Faulkner (whom Searle also admired) and Saul Steinberg. Trog loved Felix Topolski's work too, although it was too free and idiosyncratic for him to derive much benefit from its example.

There is a paradox here. Unlike Illingworth, whose style is disciplined and tight, each of these other artists cultivated a cunning casualness, a studied spontaneity of line (which looks freer and more natural that it is.) In spite of his admiration for such draughtsmen and the occasional sign of their influence in his early work Trog has never given his own style the same kind of looseness and immediacy. It might be better to say that he has never been able to endow his style with such qualities. He sometimes wishes that he could do

These rare examples of Trog roughs make a striking contrast with his finished effect

so. He believes that he has never been able to draw a satisfactory line with a brush, an instrument more likely to produce a spontaneous effect than a pen.

That Trog can be direct and spontaneous is demonstrated by the roughs for his cartoons. Drawn with a brush for the most part, they have a verve and dash absent from the finished drawings based on them. The striking contrast between the roughs and the completed cartoons may well betray an important element in the artist's personality. The roughs are essentially private: under normal circumstances the only other person ever to see them is Trog's editor. The published cartoons by contrast are, of course, entirely public. The tight, slightly self-conscious style of the latter presents a dazzlingly accomplished, technically brilliant image which reveals an insecure man anxious lest he give too much of his inner self away.

Trog satirizes the art world in two Flook
episodes

Another artist influenced Trog's early work. He was not a cartoonist but a painter
and illustrator who, during the two decades after the war, was widely regarded as one of
the best artists in England.

This was John Minton and Trog was taught illustration by him at Camberwell College
of Art, an institution dominated at the time by William Coldstream and several of his friends
from the pre-war Euston Road School which advocated a broadly Realist approach to both
style and subject-matter. Minton was anything but a Realist, however. His intricate, angular
style owed much to the English Romantic tradition of landscape painting, to the visionary
drawings and etchings of William Blake and Samuel Palmer and to the work of Minton's
near contemporary, Graham Sutherland.

Trog heard about Minton's illustration class from Humphrey Lyttleton who after the
war had decided to study at Camberwell rather than go to university. Trog also discovered
that it was possible to enroll as a part-time student. In 1947 he therefore took a day off
from the *Daily Mail* every week and spent it as a student at Camberwell.

Minton's style, with its versatile pen line, its rich repertoire of tones and textures
produced with black and white alone and its crowded but easily legible compositions, provided
Trog with an antidote to the influence of the far freer, informal and calligraphic style of
such cartoonists as Searle. Minton's drawings are those of a painter. They are, in Trog's
words, 'built, constructed'[11], exhibiting qualities of eccentric balance and a clear relationship
between the parts which quickly began to distinguish Trog's work as well.

11. *ibid.*

Trog studied at Camberwell for only a year, yet the experience made a lasting impression on him and made him wish more fervently than ever that he had been able to complete his training at Sidcup. (He now says that when he retires he is determined to return to art school). Such appreciation of the benefits of formal art training is rare among cartoonists, many of whom did not study art at all and believe that it would not have helped them if they had. Trog's interest in art in general is equally unusual and keeps breaking through in his work. In an early episode of Flook the attitudes of reactionary academicians, radical modernists and the exploitation of both by the trade are satirised and several of Trog's most memorable political cartoons have been based on masterpieces by Constable, Turner and Munch.

FLOOK

At the *Daily Mail* Trog did not produce column-breakers and other decorative graphic work for long. In 1948 he was given the opportunity to draw a new daily comic strip intended for children. The paper's proprietor, Lord Rothermere, had been impressed by 'Barnaby', an American strip about a child with a strange fairy godfather, [12] and was determined to have something like it in the *Mail*. At that moment the cartoon department of the newspaper was considering a broadly similar idea proposed by the journalist Douglas Mount who had prepared a synopsis and commissioned some sample drawings. He called his strip 'Lefty and the Goop', a title which no one in the cartoon department liked. The sample drawings were not much admired, either. Rusty became Rufus and the Goop became Flook while Trog was asked if he would like to draw the strip. Mount would provide the scripts.

The name Flook was the invention of Humphrey Lyttleton who had just been recruited to the *Mail* at Trog's suggestion. When Trog gave up producing graphics in order to concentrate on the strip, Lyttleton took over his responsibilities as a general illustrator. He illustrated readers' letters (he even wrote some of them) and eventually drew a daily pocket cartoon. Fawkes still smiles at the irony implicit in the fact that the Old Etonian former Guards captain acquired his first job not on the old-boy-network but with the aid of someone who had left his local school at the age of fourteen.

12. *'Barnaby' was the work of Crokett Johnson (David Johnson Leisk) and first appeared in 1942 in the New York newspaper* PM. *Barnaby's fairy godfather, the portly Mr O'Malley, instead of working his magic for good unintentionally caused chaos and havoc — without ever realising how inept he was. 'Barnaby' was discontinued in 1952. According to* The World Enclyclopedia of Comics *(ed. Maurice Horn, New York, 1976, p98) the strip 'was an artistic masterpiece. It contained some of the cleverest and most literate writing in comics ...' The effect of 'Barnaby' on 'Flook' was only very indirect. Its graphic style was highly simplified, almost the complete antithesis of that of 'Flook'.*

Trog began the preparatory work on Flook during 1948. The most difficult problem was the creation of Flook who had to look strange and yet be credible at the same time. Eventually he produced a drawing of a small creature with large ears, round eyes, a trunk and hair like astrakhan all over his body and the cartoon department declared itself happy with the creation. Quite quickly, but not quickly enough for changes to made, Trog realised that Flook's lack of anything like hands made it almost impossible for him to be shown holding anything.

The first strip, then called 'Rufus', was published on 25 April 1949 and told the story of an extinct, prehistoric creature who fell out of one of Rufus's nightmares into the boy's bed and who possessed the magical ability to turn into anything at will and sometimes unintentionally. Flook stayed with Rufus who, living not with his parents but with an uncle of decidedly Victorian ideas, had been longing for a friend.

Flook falls into the real world out of the dreams of Rufus (whose name his strip used to bear), and a celebrated strip-cartoon character is created

The graphic style of the early 'Rufus' stories was more unusual than their plots. Its human characters were carefully observed and differentiated, its backgrounds the obvious results of diligent research and study and its line was remarkably varied. Its narrative method was also unusually sophisticated.

For a time Flook's transformations provided much of the dramatic interest. In the first episode of all, for example, he puts out a fire with the aid of his trunk, having

turned it into a hose. Gradually, however, unusual locations and a cast of strange and even bizarre supporting characters diverted the attention somewhat from Flook's metamorphoses.

Douglas Mount provided the scripts until 1950 when another journalist, Robert Raymond, took over. He was followed by Sir Compton Mackenzie who wrote 'Rufus' for most of 1953. His successor was Humphrey Lyttleton who continued to write the strip until 1956.

The presence in that list of the name of a celebrated author — Compton Mackenzie (best-known for *Whisky Galore)* — testifies to the remarkable prestige the strip had quickly acquired. The *Mail* realised that 'Rufus' was read not only by children but also, in the words of Robert Raymond, 'by grown-ups, in Cambridge common rooms and City boardrooms, in country parsonages and Mayfair advertising agencies.'[13]

Those 'grown-ups' were attracted to the strip by the quality of its drawing, the vivid dialogue and eccentric humour, all of them unmatched by any British strip (and very few American), then or later.

Douglas Mount remembered that already during the brief period when he was producing scripts, the management 'wanted to turn the strip into a vehicle for social and political satire' and that this was the reason for his resignation: 'As far as I was concerned Flook was strictly for the kids and I couldn't visualise it any other way.'[14]

There was, however, little sign of any obvious satire for several years and Trog himself recalls that the first story to include even gentle political implications was published in 1952. It was about the abominable snowmen on Mount Everest, some of whom were thin and some were fat. In a ludicrous version of the Cold War they disputed possession of the snow supply and began to fight. Flook persuaded them to end hostilities by suggesting that they all became medium abominable snowmen. All the snowmen spoke in Pitman's shorthand in an effort to engage the interest of secretaries among the *Mail's* readers.

Political satire and social comment gradually became a major feature of the strip. At the same time the relationship between Rufus and Flook changed. Flook was always the brighter partner (he spoke several languages fluently and at least pretended to omniscience); but he was initially unthinkable without his red-haired friend, Rufus. Imperceptibly, however,

13. *quoted after Robert Raymond, 'The Man with a Flook on his Mind' in* Flook at 30, *p7*

14. *quoted after Douglas Mount, 'The Birth of Flook', in* Flook at 30, *p6-7*

he assumed the rôle of Rufus's surrogate father, amazed and frequently annoyed by the boy's ignorance and naiveté. As Flook's wisdom grew (and with it his disenchantment with the contemporary world of fashionable trends and causes), his powers of transformation waned so that eventually he was scarcely able to change himself into anything.

While Rufus remained static as a personality, his development arrested at the pre-pubescent stage, Flook's character grew. He may have been something of a sage but he was also subject to fits of pique and to periods of damaging self-love during which he was scarcely preferable to any of his narcissistic, arrogant, feckless or scheming friends and acquaintances.

The development of the relationship between Rufus and Flook was reflected by the title of the strip. 'Rufus' became 'Rufus and Flook' before ending up as 'Flook.' The final transformation of 'Flook' into a masterpiece of the art comparable to 'Pogo' and 'Li'l Abner' was the achievement of a collaboration between Trog and George Melly. Melly was another jazzman, a blues singer much influenced by Bessie Smith who, since leaving public school, had pursued a highly unconventional career as a merchant seaman and assistant to E.L.T. Mesens, the Belgian Surrealist artist and poet and London art dealer. Melly took over the writing of 'Flook' from Humphrey Lyttleton in 1956 and continued to provide scripts until 1971.

Melly's unerring eye for the spurious and fashionable as well as the large social or political issue was accompanied by his infallible ear for the suddenly illuminating heights

George Melly

George Melly and Wally Fawkes (*right*)
drawing Flook c. 1960

which, in spite of the talents of such distinguished successors as Barry Norman, Barry Took, Peter Lewis and Keith Waterhouse, it never quite managed to reach again.

The brilliance of 'Flook' during the fifteen years of Melly's involvement might be thought to demonstrate Trog's heavy reliance on his collaborators and even to suggest that he was only ever the illustrator of other people's ideas. This is far from the truth. 'Flook' was essentially his strip. He worked with the scriptwriter at every stage, reminding him of what could be expressed visually and what could not; he regularly suggested topics, themes and dialogue.

Flook's thirtieth birthday, 1979

The nature of the collaboration was once defined by Barry Norman who referred to the very occasional 'clash of integrities' between artist and writer which resulted in a problem that 'was always solved in the same way. I would compromise: which is to say that I would abandon my argument and fall in with Wally's. And this, of course, was the right and proper thing to do for, in the end, Flook is Wally's creation. Scriptwriters come and go and all of them are replaceable: Wally is not. Without him there could be no Flook.'[15]

Barry Took would agree. In his time with 'Flook' and Trog 'his were always the best jokes, the better ideas, the elegant phrase that said everything in four words. It was *his* strip after all, and his was the magic.'[16]

Writing and drawing 'Flook' was hard work. Read in a few seconds (although often remembered by the grateful reader for years), a single strip took the best part of a day

15. *quoted after Barry Norman, 'Foot and Grape' in* Flook at 30, *p14*

16. *quoted after Barry Took, 'For Fawkes Sake', in* Flook at 30, *p15*

to draw. Trog researched all the details with the obsession of a pioneering archaeologist, scouring photographic archives for the authentic object or item of dress, going on sketching expeditions on his bicycle all over London in pursuit of the right period street lamp or cobbled pavement.

When the strip began publication about three months worth of episodes had already been completed as an insurance against illness or some other disaster. But Trog's meticulous and time-consuming methods resulted in a depletion of the stock and he was eventually obliged to economise a little on detail and develop a less intricate style. The visual variety of 'Flook' was sustained, however, and the lively interplay of black, white, tone and texture within each strip continued to distinguish it from all other things of its kind.

'Flook's' graphic style was assured and mature from the first frame of the first episode, an extraordinary achievement for an artist who had never attempted to draw a strip before, let alone one who, like Trog, had never critically examined other strips to see what he could learn from them. So Trog unwittingly broke rules. Instead of roughing out each strip in pencil, having the text lettered by a specialist and then completing the drawing in ink, Trog would finish all the inking first, leaving what he thought was enough white space for the letterer. Few strip cartoonists would believe that there were not frequent disasters.

What then, if not the example of other comic strips, was responsible for the sophistication, variety and easy flow of narrative and richness of composition evident in even the earliest 'Flook' strips? The method was essentially cinematic and the inspiration came from film, specifically *Citizen Kane*, Orson Welles' masterpiece. Trog saw the movie literally scores of times, amazed by the camerawork and the montage but repeatedly bemused by the plot.

One of the characters who appeared in several episodes of 'Flook' (including one of the earliest) was the film director Orson Kaart, obviously if loosely based on the obese and self-regarding Welles. Many such characters, both major and minor, were based on real people, some of them famous, some of them Trog's friends and acquaintances and it is on their presence that much of the strip's vitality and interest depends.

Thus the permanently inebriated, strawberry-nosed journalist, George Jabb, was based on the *Daily Mirror's* chief sports writer, Peter Wilson ('The Man They Cannot Gag'), while

Eight frames from Flook involving George Jabb

Brendan Behan, George Best and a small parliament of politicians both English and American have put in regular or intermittent appearances over the years.

Many characters were based on people with less public faces, however. Len Bloggs, manager of a rock group called The Bootles was modelled on the music agent Jim Godbolt while Inspector Herbert 'Red' Herring of the Yard had the features of Julian Holland, one of Trog's colleagues on the *Daily Mail*. Those readers who recognised the models felt they belonged to an exclusive clique; those who did not responded to the vitality of the portraits which their basis in life provided.

Some characters came entirely from Trog's imagination but then began to assume the appearance and manners of real people — or perhaps it was the other way about. The best example of this process of life imitating art is Mr Muckybrass who according to George Melly 'did not start as a Harold Wilson figure: he started as a northern industrialist 'Room

Mr Muckybrass has a drink with Flook

17.   *quoted after George Melly, 'The Flook in my Life', in* Flook at 30, *p.11*

at the Top' man. He somehow assumed Wilsonian characteristics without ever looking anything like him. He *is* Wilson now ...'[17]

A similar although less obvious case concerns one of the central characters in many episodes of 'Flook' — Bodger, the epitome of the 'bovver boy' before the term was coined. Although he, too, was entirely imaginary, he provoked the wrath of the writer and former criminal Frank Norman who was convinced that Bodger was based on him. Once Trog had recognised the unwitting resemblance Bodger grew to look even more like Frank Norman.

Even Flook himself, the most imaginary character of all, has been known to assume the characteristics of a real and celebrated individual, as when, in an episode of 1974, he donned glasses, black jacket and sponge-bag trousers and took on the appearance of the famous solicitor and gourmand, Lord Goodman. A drawing which Trog dedicated to

Bodger and Moses Maggot in mediaeval guise

Goodman suggests that the subject was flattered to recognise himself in the furry, portly and sagacious star of the strip.

It is misleading to talk about 'Flook' in the past tense. The strip survives. But since it was axed by the *Daily Mail* in 1984 it has been a pale shadow of its former self. At the time the *Mail* decided to discontinue 'Flook' it was both written and drawn by Trog who had worked on his own since 1980 and who felt, unlike his masters, that there was considerable mileage left in his creation. So, evidently, did Robert Maxwell who had recently bought the *Daily Mirror* and whose wife and children had been 'Flook' enthusiasts for many years. 'Flook', expelled from Bouverie Street therefore migrated to Holborn Circus where Trog also found (or rather was given) a new collaborator in Keith Waterhouse, the *Daily Mirror* columnist, novelist and playwright. After less than a year 'Flook' ceased to appear in the paper whose readers must have been bemused by its sophistication. It lives on only in the Sunday Mirror where, relegated to a page towards the back of the paper, it has become nothing more than a two-frame political cartoon with a punchline. It is sad fate to have befallen one of the greatest strips in the history of art.

Fortunately for us Flook's classical incarnation survives in places more accessible than the newspaper section of the British Library at Colindale. There have been five book reprints of complete stories, one of them in hardback,[18] and another story, never previously reprinted, appears here. It demonstrates that 'Flook' provides as accurate a picture of the political and social fashions of the last four decades as one could possibly wish for. Historians will disregard these strips as potential source material at their peril.

For Lord Goodman .... by Trog
(after Graham Sutherland)
August 1974

18. *'The Amazing Adventures of Rufus and Flook', 'Rufus and Flook v. Moses Maggot', 'Rufus and Flook at School', 'Flook by Trog', 'Flook and the Peasants' Revolt.' There is also a mock autobiography not in strip form, 'I Flook.' The Centre for the Study of Cartoons and Caricature at the University of Kent at Canterbury preserves several thousand original drawings for 'Flook'.*

FLOOK
by TROG

FLOOK
by TROG

FLOOK
by TROG

FLOOK
by TROG

FLOOK
by TROG

FLOOK
by TROG

FLOOK by TROG

AH, FLOOK, PUSSYCAT, MEET YOUR FELLOW NOSHERS AND GRAB A DRINK. THEN WE'LL TOTTER INTO THE STUDIO

WELL, JUST A TINY ONE. I'M NOT FEELING TOO BRILLIANT REALLY AFTER A HARD DAY IN THE RESTAURANTS

TV CENTRE BAR

THIS IS PROFESSOR STUFFPOT, THE HISTORICAL EXPERT ON MEDIEVAL CUISINE

AH, I'VE JUST READ YOUR BOOK. I GATHER ST. MUG HASN'T CONVINCED YOU?

ST. MUG? *I'D* HAVE ROASTED HIM OVER A SLOW FIRE MYSELF

TV CENTRE BAR

AND AREN'T YOU BARON VON GUTT— AUTHOR OF 'HAPSBURG EATING HABITS— GLUTTONY AS A DISCIPLINE'?

YAH. IT ISS GOOT TO STUFFEN DER BELLY, NO? FOR SUPER-MAN— SUPER-TUM!

TIME TO GO TO THE STUDIO, CHAPS, AND REMEMBER, TALK WITH YOUR MOUTHS FULL

I DON'T FEEL MY BEST AT ALL

STUDIO 4

5133

FLOOK by TROG

I'D BETTER WATCH FLOOK'S PROGRAMME, I SUPPOSE

IT'S ALL HE THINKS ABOUT THESE DAYS

THE GREEDY HOUR

GOOD EVENING. IN THIS AGE OF BROILER FACTORIES AND FROZEN FOOD, WE FEEL THAT EATING NEEDS RESCUING. ON THIS PROGRAMME EACH WEEK...

...I AND MY FELLOW GOURMETS ARE GOING TO TRY TO MAKE YOUR MOUTHS WATER...I FEEL DREADFUL

AH, DELICIOUS BORTSCH. PERHAPS THE CREAM ISN'T QUITE SOUR ENOUGH

5134

FLOOK by TROG

...WELL, AFTER THE BORSCH AND THE SALMON TART AND CHICKEN LIVER PATE...

...IT IS TIME FOR SOMETHING MORE SUBSTANTIAL

I THINK I'M GOING TO PASS OUT.

WAITER! MORE WINE

STOP! *STOP!* YOU'RE TURNING INTO PIGS!

DON'T BE SO DAMNED RUDE

SWINEHUND!

5135

TV

FLOOK
by TROG

CAN WE GO TO THE PICTURES TONIGHT, FLOOK?

NO. IT'S A DOUBLE-F FEATURE AT THE LOCAL

BESIDES, I'VE GOT TO WATCH TV ALL EVENING FOR THE 'NO GRUB ON TV SOCIETY'

NOW GO AND INGEST YOUR GLASS OF COW-JUICE, BOILED HEN-FRUIT AND ONE SLICE OF B. AND B.

CAN I EAT IT HERE BY THE TELLY?

NO. BESIDES, BBC 8½ IS ON. IT'S AN ADULT PROGRAMME AT THE BEST OF TIMES

...AND NOW, KEN, AS LIGHTING ADVISOR TO THE NATIONAL DOCUMENTARY FILM UNIT, WHAT ARE YOUR VIEWS ON THE NEW ANTI-NOURISHMENT LAWS?

FLOOK
by TROG

NOW THE POINT IS, KEN, IF YOUR DOCUMENTARY FILM UNIT WAS MAKING A FILM ABOUT—ER—ORALLY INGESTED—ER—NOURISHMENT—ER—

NOTHING WRONG UP UNTIL NOW. IT IS A MATTER OF ADULT CONCERN EXPRESSED IN PERFECTLY GOOD TASTE

...WOULD YOU THINK IT RIGHT TO SHOW THIS ON THE SCREEN?

LOOK, MOST SENSIBLE ADULT PEOPLE ARE NOT OUTRAGED BY THE—ER—WORD—ER—

—FOOD

'FOOD'! HE USED THE WORD 'FOOD' ON TELEVISION...

THE BBC IS ENGAGED ALL THE TIME. THOUSANDS OF PROTESTING VIEWERS, NO DOUBT. I KNOW, I'LL GO ROUND AND SEE MUCKYBRASS IMMEDIATELY

FLOOK
by TROG

YES, AS ADVISER TO THE MINISTER FOR DEPRIVATION AND SELF-SACRIFICE IT'S MY DUTY TO TELL MUCKYBRASS AT ONCE THAT THE WORD 'FOOD' HAS BEEN USED ON TELLY

BUT MEANWHILE AT DOWNING STREET...

'EVENING, CABINET. I'VE ASKED YOU ALL TO COME ROUND THIS EVENING TO TELL YOU SUMMAT, BUT FIRST, 'OW ABOUT SUMMAT TO EAT?

TO EAT? IN PUBLIC? I THOUGHT THAT WAS AGAINST MORALITY AND ECONOMIC NATIONAL INTERESTS

AYE, IT WERE, BUT THE SQUEEZE IS OVER. WE NEED A BOOM NOW, SO WE MUST ENCOURAGE FOLK TO STUFF 'EMSELVES AGAIN

FLOOK
by TROG

BUT, ST. MUG, DON'T GO! IT'S NOT ENOUGH TO BE AGAINST EATING BECAUSE YOU DON'T LIKE IT ANY MORE

MUST GO, DEAR BOY. I'M GUEST ON THE *ST. PETER'S SHOW*. THEY'VE GOT ME OPPOSITE ST. CRUMPET, PATRON SAINT OF PASTRY COOKS...

5|66

I'M EVER SO HUNGRY, FLOOK. IS IT TIME TO FIND SOME BRUISED FRUIT AND OLD CABBAGE LEAVES?

IT IS *NOT*, RUFUS

IT IS TIME TO GO HOME, HAVE A NICE BATH... AND THEN...

GO OUT AND SPEND A TINY FORTUNE IN THE EATING HOUSES OF SOHO

Eleven years after starting work on 'Flook' Trog began to broaden his artistic range. In 1959 he was asked to contribute political cartoons to the *Spectator*, the Conservative weekly then edited by Brian Inglis. It was not Inglis but the art editor, Rory McEwan (yet another combination of artist and musician), who suspected that Trog's talents might flourish further if released from the confines of a strip. The artist was enthusiastic but feared that he could only succeed with the help of George Melly, then his collaborator on 'Flook' and a man of firm, if by the Spectator's standards widely left-wing opinions. Trog says that he had too scant a notion of politics at the time — 'I hadn't done the reading' [19] — and lacked confidence in his ability to produce suitable ideas for the drawings.

Melly was keen to collaborate and Trog began to address the problem of caricature for the first time. Basing characters in 'Flook' on real people was one thing, drawing politicians on a larger scale so that their facial expressions and gestures were made to carry a message was quite another.

Studying Vicky's work proved an invaluable help. This may sound unlikely. After all, Vicky's brush-drawn, apparently casual and stenographic manner is the antithesis of Trog's carefully structured, disciplined style. But it was precisely Vicky's ability to achieve the essence of a personality in a spontaneous, short-hand image — what Trog describes as 'the rhythm of the thing' [20] — which taught him how to look for and pin down the idiosyncratic details of a face and posture on which all successful caricature depends.

Trog's weekly cartoon appeared in the *Spectator* for three years, a period during which Trog also began to contribute occasionally to *Private Eye*, relishing the unique opportunity the magazine provided to disregard all conventional rules of taste and decorum. Trog then moved to the *New Statesman*, the leading weekly of the intellectual left with a higher circulation than the *Spectator*. Vicky was the *Statesman*'s political cartoonist at the time and Trog was asked to concentrate on social issues. He was also given rather more space.

The editor who pursuaded Trog to join the *Statesman* was John Freeman. Three years later he was succeeded by Paul Johnson who quickly let Trog know that he was unhappy

19. *Interview*

20. *ibid.*

Private Eye, 1966

21. *The* Observer *was about to lose its political cartoonist, Abu, who had decided to return to India.*

22. *Interview*

with the cartoon. The artist misinterpreted the criticism, thought he had been dismissed and immediately signed a contract with the *Observer*, whose editor, David Astor had been pursuing him for some time.[21] When, a week later, Johnson telephoned Trog to ask where the cartoon was since the deadline was fast approaching, Trog replied: 'It's in the *Observer*.'[22]

With the exception of the years between 1968 and 1971 Trog's work has been published in the *Observer* ever since and his editorial and pocket cartoons remain two of the Sunday paper's most distinguished features.

In 1968 Leslie Illingworth retired as the *Daily Mail's* senior political cartoonist and advised the editor to offer his job to Trog. Trog was excited by the prospect of producing several cartoons a week and now felt able to work on his own, without the ideas of George Melly which, the *Mail* had in any case announced, were not likely to be to its taste.

The partnership (which continued to produce 'Flook') was dissolved without rancour. Melly was already enjoying a flourishing career as a writer. Indeed, it was 'Flook' which made Melly — and newspaper editors — realise that he could write. He has since combined a highly visible career as a jazz singer (with John Chilton's Feetwarmers) with his writing. He also continues to collaborate with a cartoonist: it is Melly who gives Marc the ideas for his pocket cartoon in the *Daily Telegraph*.

When the time arrived for Trog to start work he was dismayed to discover that the *Mail's* proprietor, Lord Rothermere, had given Gerald Scarfe the job which Trog had assumed was his.

Scarfe was a young, very original caricaturist whose savage, often scatalogical and wildly distorted drawings were then appearing in *Private Eye* and had brought him fame. There were many reasons why his work was unsuitable for a popular newspaper with a predominantly middle-class readership: it purposely offended conventional taste; its targets were indiscriminately chosen and its style depended on distortions so extreme that only the visually educated could recognise the subjects of the caricatures.

Scarfe's methods were, moreover, laborious and slow. They required more time than the production of a daily newspaper allowed. Also Scarfe is essentially a caricaturist, seemingly unable to conceive the kind of ideas on which a political cartoon depends. It rapidly became clear that his appointment was a mistake. Even though Scarfe modified (some would say ruined) his style in an attempt to keep to the daily deadline and even though Bernard Levin was engaged to provide him with ideas, Scarfe alienated readers. He was given special projects — for example an assignment in Vietnam — to work out his contract while Trog was finally able to take over as the *Mail's* senior political cartoonist.

Trog now worked alone. The years working with Melly had been crucial. They had taught Trog how to select and think about subjects in a way that could find direct visual expression and powerfully express his own political point of view. That point of view is

23. *Foreword to* Trogshots, *London, 1984,*
unpaginated

broadly liberal, broadly left and cannot be categorised with the aid of any political label. George Melly once described Trog's stance as 'on the anti-Marxist left … he longs for a fair and stable society in which reason governs … He is a pessimist politically, and there who can blame him?'[23] Trog is concerned more with issues, with the effects of policies than with the policies themselves and he has been moved to anger as much by the demagogues of the left, by Benn and Scargill, as by the smug self-righteousness of the right.

At the *Daily Mail* Trog purposely changed his graphic style. In order to get away from the tight appearance of Illingworth's work and the consciously precious line of Emmwood (who also drew regularly for the paper) Trog started to paint his cartoons, using gouache to produce what art historians know as *grisailles*, tonal paintings using only black, white and a variety of greys. The results, unique in the history of the political cartoon, were extraordinarily effective.

'Now there's *real* progress — his father used to be a butler here' *Daily Mail,* 1969

Such a technique is not, at least in theory, appropriate to letterpress reproduction on newsprint which tends to blur half-tones and Trog was able to work in this way only because the *Mail's* blockmakers were so good. When he was back at the *Observer* he had to abandon the technique because the blockmakers there proved less resourceful and sensitive than their colleagues at the *Mail*.

It was in 1971 that Trog returned to the *Observer* whose editor, dissatisified with Richard Wilson (Trog's successor three years before) had been trying to win Trog back for some time. When David English became the *Mail's* editor in 1971 he set about changing the character of the entire paper, to take it down market, to increase its appeal to women and younger readers and, not least, to reduce its format from broadsheet to tabloid. As part of this policy he did away with political cartoons entirely and gave the *Mail's* major cartoon spot to Mac, the social commentator then working for the *Mail's* sister paper, the *Daily Sketch*. Trog's services were no longer required (other than as the artist of 'Flook') and he was free to return to the *Observer*.

On the day that Trog's contract with the *Mail* ended William Davis, the editor of *Punch*, invited him to draw the magazine's weekly full-page political cartoon. Until then Trog's association with *Punch* had not extended beyond the production of an occasional full-colour cover and Davis's invitation reflected the stature that the artist had achieved as a political cartoonist. The big cartoon in *Punch* was the highest ambition to which any cartoonist in Britain could aspire. Once again Trog was following in the footsteps of Leslie Illingworth.

Trog's awareness of the tradition which he now continued is reflected in the elaborate drawing style which he developed for *Punch*. Although he continued intermittently to paint his cartoons in gouache he now increasingly used pen and ink alone to produce dense cross-hatching reminiscent of the effects producd by the Victorian engravers. Indeed, Trog's *Punch* cartoons allude in subject-matter as well as style not only to the work of such immediate predescessors as Illingworth but also such nineteenth-century masters as Tenniel.

The weight of tradition proved crushingly heavy. Like the entire British press *Punch* was changing. The ideas for the major political cartoon, produced as always by an editorial committee sitting around the famous table (for which purpose it had originally been installed), were too often out of tune with the times and the issues with which the committee felt the

'Picking up another pilot' *Punch*, 1973.
Both this and facing illustration pay homage to
John Tenniel, an earlier *Punch* cartoonist

'Dropping the pilot' *Punch*, 1976

London Daily News, 1987

cartoon ought to be concerned often seemed inflated when addressed in so elaborate a fashion.

Trog himself was in part responsible for bringing the tradition to an end. At one of the committee meetings in 1974 he declared the cartoon to be an anachronism and suggested that *Punch* ceased to publish it. The committee agreed, the tradition ended and has not been revived. Although Trog continues occasionally to provide colour covers and, more often, portrait drawings for *Punch*, for twelve years his political cartoons appeared only in the *Observer*.

Then, in 1986, Trog joined the new colour tabloid *Today*, leaving it after only a few months for the new evening paper, the *London Daily News*, then in its protracted planning

Today, 1986

THE OBSERVER —

Observer, 1975

24. *quoted after James Cameron, foreword to*
The World of Trog, *London, 1977, p5*

stage. That paper began and ceased publication in 1987 and Trog's political cartoons are once again confined to the *Observer* for the time being.

The differences between the production of a comic strip and an editorial cartoon are as obvious as they are enormous. The strip cartoonist works several weeks, often months in advance; he draws to a script and his major problems derive from the demands of a continuous narrative and restricted space. Within the few square centimetres of a single frame he must accommodate not only figures and background but also dialogue. The text must be easily legible and combined with the drawing in a clear and visually stimulating composition. If the reader is to be carried along the composition of each frame within each strip must relate to but be different from the next.

The editorial cartoonist on the other hand can never work more than a day or two in advance if his ideas are to remain topical and fresh. (Trog usually draws his cartoon for the Sunday *Observer* on the previous Friday.) Unlike the strip cartoonist, however, he has the advantage of generous space and fewer words. The effect of the political cartoon is instant and direct, not cumulative. It affords the opportunity both for great detail and bold, dramatic contrasts of form and tone.

It is impossible to say how Trog — or any other cartoonist for that matter — produces his ideas. The best of them simply come in a process so natural that it defies analysis, while even the idea that arrives only after long thought cannot be explained in any logical terms. Trog himself once put it this way: 'You read the news and give yourself the subject-matter for the cartoon. You decide that this is the story of the week and you read all the papers. You begin to get feelings about it. Whose side are you on? Is this right? Is this fair? This is the sort of gut-feeling you have. You wait for the digestive phase, then with any luck the answer comes floating to the surface, and you start to draw.'[24]

Inevitably some ideas are better than others and it can be argued that the very best of Trog's work contrives to make a memorable statement in terms of a visual image alone — or at any rate with a minimum of text. Thus the millions of dollars which President Ford was profligately pouring into Cambodia in 1975 are arranged in the form of a funeral wreath while, seven years later, the crosses marking the grave of the fallen during the Falklands War assume a form which comments bitterly on the British victory. Cartoons such as these bear comparison with the best work of Vicky, Low and even Daumier.

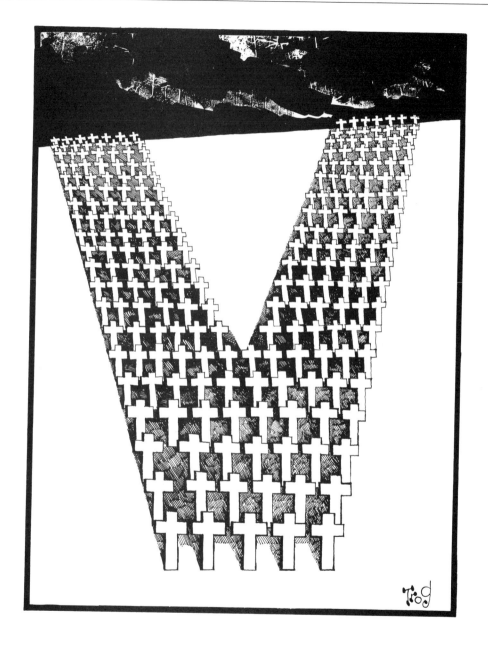

Observer, 1982

The Bishop of Woolwich's book is felt to be
more embarrassing than D.H. Lawrence's

'I don't know if it's a coincidence, but all my special clients are Tory MPs'

'But that's just it, Father, I haven't had a safe period again'

'I'm going to offer you a choice. Will you go to prison or join the police?

The mould that Mrs Thatcher broke

'Don't feel you have to fly back *each day* to report, Prime Minister'
Harold Wilson enjoys a close relationship with the Queen, but does she with him?

(*Opposite*) **'He's lucky, I had to ask Baldwin'**
The Windsors compare divorce proceedings

'It does make one more hopeful about a Middle East solution'
A Beefeater comments on the thawing of relations between the Queen and the Duke and
Duchess of Windsor

'I forgot to turn off George Brown!'
Harold Wilson panics en route to the Scillies at the thought of leaving behind his accident-prone second-in-charge

'Put that comic away, you're here to look at the pictures'
The Roy Lichtenstein exhibition opens in London

Tall left-wing actress Vanessa Redgrave is taken into custody after a CND sit-down

(*Opposite*) South Africa refuses to accept Basil D'Oliviera as a member of the MCC touring party

An air force deal between France and America leaves Wilson fuming

Enoch Powell's views on immigration as
expressed at the Tory Party Conference have not
gone unnoticed

'Mr Adair — is that you?'
The famous American oil-well trouble shooter is summoned by Edward Heath to deal with incendiary utterances by Enoch Powell

'I expect it helps them tell each other apart'
Swinging gets under way in the swinging sixties

'What do you mean, I'm putty in Vic Feather's hands? I'm putty in my *own* hands'

Wilson fails to get Cabinet backing for a senior colleague's policy — Barbara Castle's *In Place of Strife* — and his credibility as a Prime Minister is seriously damaged

'Well Paddy, and what do you expect from such a Godless city?'

'It's just as well they believe in the same God'

Trog
August 1969 'DAILY MAIL'

The British army moves into Ulster, a new
theatre of 'peace-keeping' activity

Motorway madness

'Barbara Castle has won the hair-do of the year award'
Barbara Castle's allegedly reconciliatory proposals on industrial relations, issued as *In Place of Strife*,
seem hostile to TUC secretary Vic Feather

'One small step for man'
Laos, Vietnam, Cambodia ... where next?

(*Left*) The Apollo 13 Moon mission runs into
major trouble while in Earth orbit. After Durer

'No, no, Chummy, you misunderstand — we want you *for* the police'
Persuading members of racial minorities into the police force proves a difficult task

(*Right*) Lord Snowdon wonders if his brother-in-law shouldn't be known as Prince Philip of Philistine

1970

Mary Whitehouse is stunned by the nudity as one of the classics of permissiveness reaches television

(*Left*) A recently victorious Edward Heath attends the Tory Party Conference

(*Right*) Child soldier, south-east Asia

PUNCH 11–17 NOVEMBER 1970
2s 6d (12½ np.) WEEKLY

Punch

This Week:

FIVE YEARS AFTER UDI

Ian Smith, leader of unilaterally independent Rhodesia, in pensive mood

'It won't affect him — he's been on double Scottish time for years'
The introduction of permanent 'double summer time' proved temporary after Scottish protests about dark winter mornings

'But it's the only sort of work I know'

" 'Ow much, m'sieur – 'ow much do you 'ave?"

(*Opposite*) Geoffrey Rippon and President Pompidou negotiate British entry into the Common Market

'Would you mind switching that off while I do this?'

'And we only came here to get away from Harold Wilson'
Tax exiles lose another haven

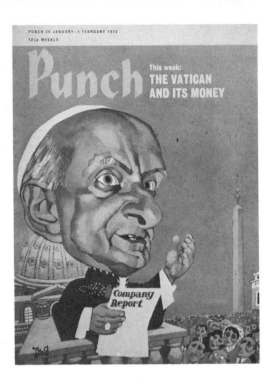

Pope Paul VI's initiatives on Vatican finance
pave the way for later troubles

'So much for your advanced technology'
President Pompidou's visit to Edward Heath coincides with national power cuts

Ted Heath's incomes policy neglects a more important target

'You don't think it could be misunderstood?'
Nixon's old presidential campaigning slogan could be unfortunate as the Watergate affair breaks,
thinks Pat

Revelations of financial malpractice by Vice-
president Spiro Agnew bring about his
resignation at the height of the Watergate affair

'Trial run'
A modern Nebuchadnezzar and his fiery
furnace

After the Watergate enquiry starts, Richard
Nixon eats his words

The Labour Party's financial policies as disclosed in the run-up to the General Election seem to have less and less to do with making pips squeak

Heath's short-lived 1974 administration —
elected in February, but back to the country in
October — looks precarious

Henry Kissinger has trouble being subservient
to President Ford

'Sorry we've got to go, Mum, but he wants to see it in colour'
New technology threatens the spirit of Christmas

In Blackpool an industrial exhibition coincides
with the Labour Party Conference

Harold Wilson and James Callaghan visit
Moscow as Labour's long-standing leadership
starts to seem superannuated but entrenched

Franco's death signals the road to recovery in Spain

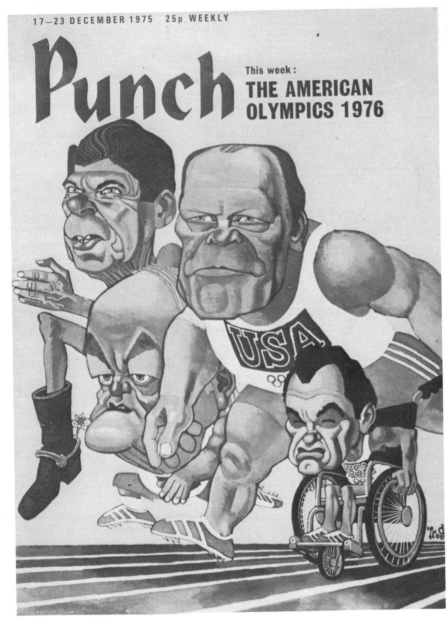

(*Right*) The Winter Olympics of 1976
— the descent of Jeremy Thorpe

(*Left*) The presidential hopefuls for 1976.
Where, you may ask, is Jimmy Carter?

BEHIND EVERY GREAT MAN …

'Behind every great man…'
Behind Jimmy Carter there are three

Carter gets the presidency, but Kissinger keeps the world

The cartoonist looks under the Red bed in response to Brezhnev's speech, during a visit to Prague, about 'absurd Western fairy-tales' of 'the bloodthirsty Soviet wolf' and 'helpless Little Red Ridinghood' Yugoslavia.

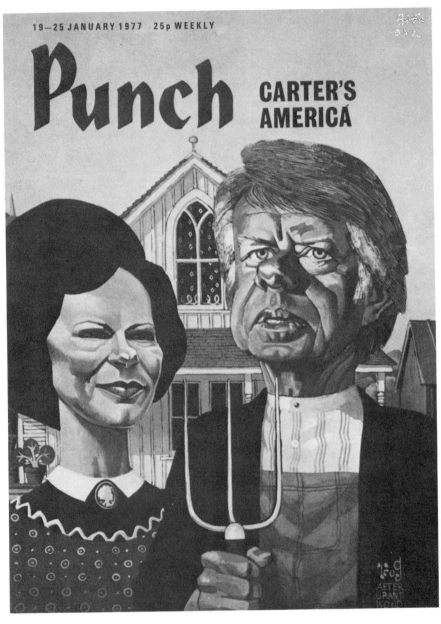

Jimmy and Rosalind Carter as the Iowan
rustics of Grant Wood's '*American Gothic*'

Ian Smith warms himself at the old anti-Whitehall fire as he fights a majority-based Rhodesia settlement — but the company has changed. After Arthur Rackham

Three thousand striking toolroom workers bring the whole of British Leyland to a standstill

Mrs Gandhi, after five months of the 'state of emergency', concedes elections

In Russia, the posts of General Secretary of
the Central Committee of the party and
President of the Praesidium are combined for
the first time

The Queen celebrates her Silver Jubilee to the
sound of her tune

Menachim Begin thwarts Sadat's peace initiatives
in the Middle East

The Tartan Army shows political nous on the
way to the World Cup

Listeners to the newly broadcast Prime Minister's Question Time on BBC Radio think it should be renamed 'On Your Farm'

It is 1979, and the Queen is already
anticipating some role reversal

The race for leadership of the Labour Party
gets under way

More top earners from the royal stable

The visit of an overseas rugby touring team to
South Africa *is* a political question

"There's already A Gang of Three — it's called The Liberal Party'

BLACKPOOL

Defections from the right-wing of the Labour Party to form a new grouping are becoming a reality

The parent-organization of the SDP — the
Council for Social Democracy — is set up
following the Limehouse Declaration

Tony Benn and Denis Healey contest the
deputy leadership of the Labour Party, as
Martin Scorsese's new film reaches Britain

British Rail's new Advanced Passenger Train is
taken out of service after proving as resistant
to turning corners as Margaret Thatcher

The Labour Party holds a council-of-war at Bishop's Stortford in an unconvincing attempt to heal its deep divisions

Norman Tebbit modernizes Saatchi and
Saatchi's 1979 election poster

After seeing the Prime Minister through the
Zimbabwe problem Foreign Secretary Lord
Carrington is ditched en route to the Falklands
— and Bogart does not get his Hepburn

Shortly after the Falklands War, Britain and Argentina meet in the semi-finals of the World Cup, providing echoes of the Christmas Day football match between British and German soldiers during the First World War

A policeman on duty at the Commons adopts the famous words of BBC correspondent Brian Hanrahan as the Cabinet go back to work after the Falklands adventure

The Unilateralist

'Come on, Denis, I'll never get down again without your extra weight'

Denis Healey refuses to get carried away by the unilateralist argument, but allows Michael Foot to be

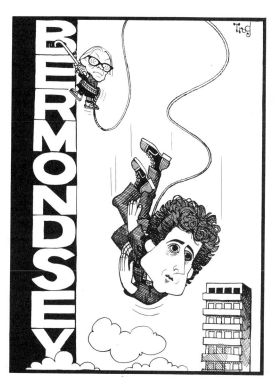

Gay radical Labour candidate in the Bermondsey by-election Peter Tatchell threatens to have a depressing effect on Michael Foot's chances in the General Election

Prince William wows them down under on his 1983 Australian tour

President Botha introduces some political rights
for South Africa's 'coloured' population, but
none for blacks

The Queen has been expressing disquiet over
excessive media attention

Chancellor Lawson updates an old slogan

Mrs Thatcher gets a less than rapturous farewell from her wet colleagues in the EEC

Hatred permeates every part of family life during the year-long coal strike

President Reagan manages to stay awake
during his inaugural address

NUM leader Arthur Scargill aims to bring
down the government with the strike in the
coalfields

Botha's law

Prince Charles and Mrs Thatcher are not thought to see eye to eye on law and order and the inner cities

Prince Charles has been publicly enthusiastic about the Land of the Free while on a trip to America

The future is nuclear — including the bodies

The growth of French neo-fascism causes more doubts to arise over the French connection

Kurt Waldheim tries to obliterate his Nazi past

Sir Geoffrey Howe is made to feel less than
welcome on his fact-finding tour of South
Africa

Norman Tebbit attempts to stifle the BBC after accusing them of anti-Tory bias. After Eric Gill's 'Prospero and Miranda' mural sculpture on the corporation's headquarters

Margaret Thatcher skirts round the Westland crisis with the same ease as Charles Addams' famous *New Yorker* skier, to Opposition dismay

Ronald Reagan doesn't seem to share Mrs Thatcher's skiing skills. After Charles Addams

Prince Edward resigns from the Marines and makes his father cross

'The snow-flakes grew bigger and bigger until they looked like great white hens. All at once they swerved to one side, the great sledge pulled up, and up stood the driver with fur coat and hat made of pure snow: it was a lady, tall and proud and dazzlingly white — she was the SNOW QUEEN'

Hans Andersen

Mrs Thatcher's heating allowance hand-out
keeps pensioners alive until after the election

Guinness scandal causes panic in the City

As Mrs Thatcher gets ever more paranoid
about what her subjects should be allowed to
know, the old couple at the centre of Raymond
Briggs' anti-nuclear cartoon book and film
When the Wind Blows are bundled away

Two world leaders share a thought

Margaret Thatcher's pre-election display of
world statesmanship in Moscow is designed to
receive rapturous applause

Mrs Thatcher denies that pre-election
government spending has anything to do with
winning votes

Presidential candidate Gary Hart borrows a line from Ronald Reagan

President Botha fails to notice that his
pressure-cooker has no safety valve

Riding high in the polls in the run-up to the 1987 election, Margaret Thatcher doesn't want underdogs to have their day

Margaret Thatcher names the election date and the sun disappears for the rest of the summer

The National Health and other services are safe in Tory hands, until they can't be patched any more

Dr Owen rejects overtures from the Liberals; Ken
Livingstone and the newly elected London left
reject overtures from Neil Kinnock

Ken Livingstone's maiden speech in the
Commons on shady activities by the Army and
Intelligence in Ulster breaks Tam
Dalyell's monopoly on Tory scandals

The American edition of *Spycatcher* reaches
the Thatcher household ahead of the returning
Prime Minister

George Melly

There is yet another kind of work at which the versatile Trog excells and which this book celebrates: portaiture. The word may sound too elevated for anything produced by a cartoonist; but the dividing line between caricature and portrait is exceedingly thin and all of Trog's work is distinguished by qualities which all conventional portraits should possess but rarely do.

Trog knows how to tread the tightrope between the straight likeness and the exaggerated lampoon. To occupy as extreme a position as Scarfe or Steadman is relatively easy, for the omnivorous misanthropy absolves the artist from distinguishing between the thoroughly evil person and the merely inept. It is infinitely harder to portray someone both humorously and with affection. It is harder still to do so and at the same time reveal something of the subject's personality.

It is not simply the fact that the subject of a Trog portrait is instantly recognisable, although the artist's knack of fastening on to the particular and the peculiar in a face or gesture seems miraculous. Trog's portraits go beyond mere physical resemblance to touch on something spiritual and emotional. The set of Lech Walesa's mouth, the furrows in his brow and the narrowing eyes express shrewdness and determination while hinting at the embattled position in which he finds himself. The more open, lighter pen drawing of Richard Burton is similarly incisive, presenting a devasting image of a man disillusioned by wealth and fame and ravaged by the effects of alcohol. It is not, strictly speaking, a caricature. It is a portrait in which the actual appearance of its subject is brought to life through the sympathy and sensitivity of the artist. Drawn from photographs, as are all of Trog's portraits, it is far more eloquent than any photograph can be.

Even more memorable than Trog's portrait drawings are his portrait paintings, many of which have appeared on the cover of *Punch*. They are produced in a way which the Old Masters would have understood. When Trog began to produce such work for *Punch*, one of the magazine's other cartoonists, Geoffrey Dickinson, lent him a book explaining the techniques of the past and suggested that Trog might benefit from studying them. Although Trog employs neither tempera nor oil but coloured gouache on board or paper, he proceeds

Carl Giles, in Trog's virtuoso gouache technique

much as Van Eyck and Michelangelo would have done, building up the flesh tints from scumbles and glazes of a small number of colours. He begins with viridian, establishing the forms of the hands and face with the aid of darker and lighter mixtures of this colour. The he applies transparent layers of burnt sienna (sometimes burnt umber) over the top until he achieves the flesh colour he requires. Finally he applies white to provide the highlights.

It is a laborious but extraordinarily effective method characteristic of an accomplished craftsman who seems unconcerned that so much time and devotion is being lavished on something which will appear only once in an ephemeral publication.

Inevitably, the best-known of Trog's portraits whether drawn or printed, are those of the Royal Family. Nowadays every cartoonist attempts now and again 'to do the Royals' but when Trog first included HM the Queen in one of his cartoons for the *Spectator* he was treading on thin ice: the subject had been considered off-limits to cartoonists for a century or more.

By comparison with the savage three-dimensional caricatures of the Royal Family made for the television show *Spitting Image*, Trog's versions of the Queen, Prince Philip, the Prince and Princess of Wales are striking for their close resemblance to the people themselves. They are well-mannered, even benign. When they appear in cartoons it is not so much they who are the target as something or, more usually, somebody else. Thus the Queen

London Daily News, 1987

is used to raise alarm about Mrs Thatcher's own seemingly monarchial pretensions. In one of the many disputes between Buckingham Palace and the press about intrusions into the Royal Family's private life by photographers, Trog leaves us in no doubt where he stands.

Wally Fawkes — Trog — is not merely one of the best political cartoonists at work anywhere in the world today, he is also one of the most versatile and best *artists.* If he had only ever drawn 'Flook' he would be remembered. If had only ever produced a weekly political cartoon for the *Observer* he would rank as one of the outstanding practitioners of the genre during the post-war period. And it can be argued that his portraits are far superior to anything among the acres of near-likenesses which annually litter the walls of the Royal Academy Summer exhibition.

Forty years is a long time in cartooning; but since Trog's work has grown consistently better during those four decades, the time is not nearly long enough. I look forward to writing about Trog's next forty graphic years in 2027.

FRANK WHITFORD

(*Overleaf*) H U G H   H E F N E R   1971

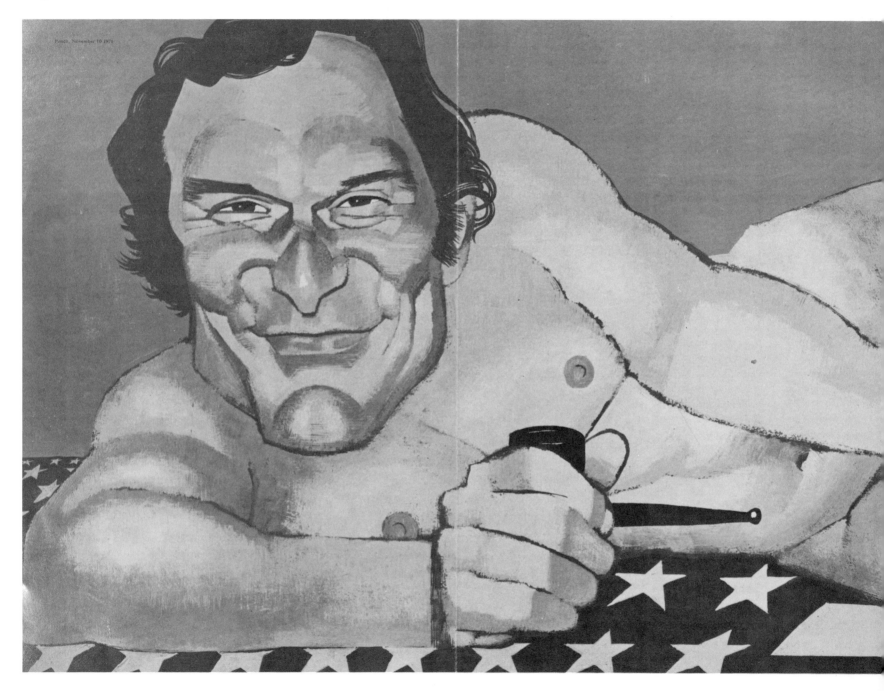

Punch, November 10 1971

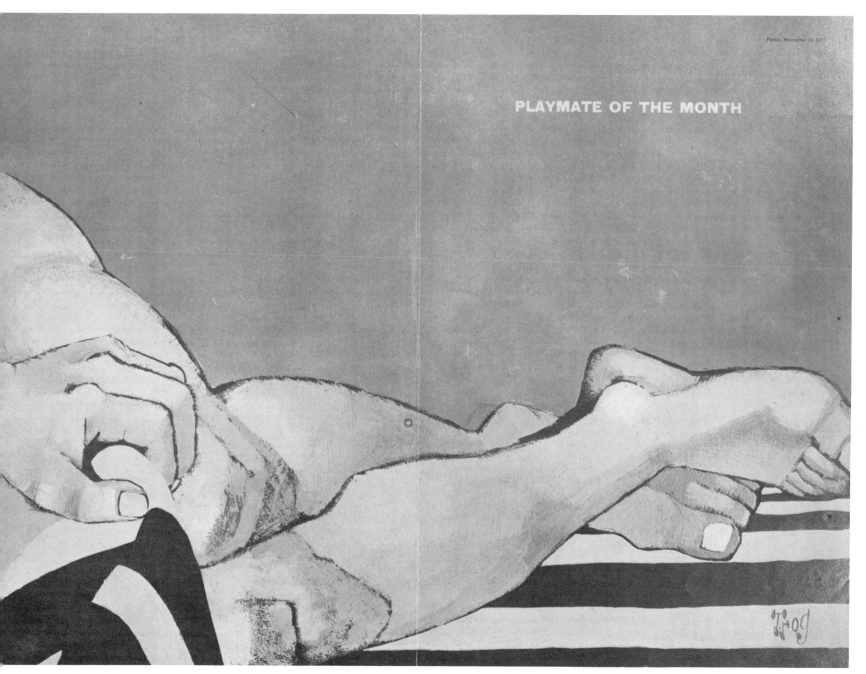

PLAYMATE OF THE MONTH

Punch, November 10 1971

FRANK SINATRA 1971

RICHARD BURTON
AND LIZ TAYLOR 1971

HUMPHREY LYTTLETON 1973

ILIE NASTASE
AND BILLIE-JEAN KING 1973

JOHN WAYNE 1974

TED HEATH 1974

MARGARET THATCHER 1975

REGINALD BOSANQUET 1978

GENE WILDER 1978   BILLY GRAHAM 1978

KEN DODD 1978

KATHERINE HELMOND 1979

GLENDA JACKSON 1980

HENRY WINKLER *(alias The Fonz)*
1980

ANDY WARHOL 1980

ALEXANDER HAIG 1981

SHIRLEY WILLIAMS 1981

BRIAN JOHNSTON 1981

MALCOLM MUGGERIDGE 1981

ROBERT MORLEY 1981

MOHAMMED ALI 1981

BILLY CONNOLLY 1982

GEORGE ORWELL
AND EVELYN WAUGH 1981

BARBARA WOODHOUSE 1982

JOHN MORTIMER 1984

PEGGY LEE 1984

DIRK BOGARDE 1984

BARBRA STREISAND 1982

ELLA FITZGERALD 1984

ROBERT MAXWELL 1984

ANDREW LLOYD WEBBER 1985

CHARLES BRONSON 1985

PUNCH May 29 1985

NORMAN TEBBIT 1985

SIR ROY STRONG 1985

RICHARD BRANSON 1986

GEORGE COLE
(*alias Arthur Daley*) 1986

SOPHIA LOREN 1986

TOM JONES 1987

PAUL NEWMAN 1987

LENNY HENRY 1987

JEFFREY ARCHER 1987

ENOCH POWELL 1987

NORMAN ST JOHN STEVAS
date unknown

GEOFFREY HOWE *date unknown*

WILLIE WHITELAW (*date unknown*)

TONY BENN *date unknown*

MARY WHITEHOUSE *date unknown*

MEL BROOKS *date unknown*